SPALDEEN

SPALDEEN
Poems

HENRY M. SEIDEN

IPBOOKS.net
International Psychoanalytic Books

International Psychoanalytic Books (IPBooks),
30-27 33rd Street, #3R
Astoria, NY 11102
Online at: www.IPBooks.net

Spaldeen: Poems
Copyright © 2016 by Henry M. Seiden

All rights reserved. No part of this book may be used or reproduced in any manner whatsoever including Internet usage, without written permission of the author.

"Men Say Brown," "Certain Death," "Tinnitus," "Unknown Soldiers," and three of the four poems "From an Analyst's Notebook" appeared in *Poetry*.

"The Heart Is Not the Red It Is Supposed To Be" and *"Approaching a city, 1946"* were published in *Literal Latte*.

"Looking For Lola" and "Theology" appeared in *The Writing Path, II*, edited by Michael Pettit, U of Iowa Press, 1996.

"Turtle Story" was in *Roots and Flowers*, Edited by Liz Rosenberg, Henry Holt, 2001.

"What Is It About Water" was in *Mercy of Tides: poems for a beach house*. Edited by Margot Wizansky, Salt Marsh Pottery Press, 2003.

"The Story As I Understand It Is" appeared in *The Humanist*.

"Haircut" was in *Passager*. "Acceptance Speech" won honorable mention in *Passager*'s 2006 poetry contest.

Five poems: "Tinnitus," "The Story As I Understand It Is," "Theological Countertransference," "Looking For Lola," and "Kumquats" appeared in *The Writing Path 2: poetry and prose from writer's conferences*, Edited by Michael Pettit, U of Iowa Press.

"Turtle Story" and "Monty" appeared in *Roots & Flowers*, Edited by Liz Rosenberg, Holt, NY, 2001.

"Pictures My Mother Left Me" was published in *Psychoanalytic Perspectives* in 2010.

Many of these poems are in a chapbook called *Tinnitus*, Good Books Editions, 2009.

Book design by Maureen Cutajar
www.gopublished.com

Library of Congress Control Number: 2016954761
ISBN: 978-0-9969996-5-6

For all my teachers

About the Author

HENRY M. SEIDEN, PH.D. ABPP is a psychologist and psychoanalyst who lives and practices in Forest Hills, New York.

He is the author of *The Motive for Metaphor: brief essays on poetry and psychoanalysis* published by Karnac Books in 2016 and has published a poetry chapbook called *Tinnitus*.

He has published poetry in a number of journals including *Poetry, Literal Latte, Passager, Midstream, The Humanist* and the *Journal of the American Medical Association*. He has an essay in *Poet Lore* called "Home Thoughts." His published professional papers include articles on Wallace Stevens, on Ernest Hemingway, on the Longing for Home, on metaphor, on using poetry in psychotherapy with children among other subjects.

He is co-author (with Christopher Lukas) of *Silent Grief: living in the wake of suicide* (which was originally published by Scribners, 1988, and is now with Jessica Kingsley.) It has been translated into Chinese, Portuguese and Russian.

Seiden is a member the Board of Editors of *Psychoanalytic Psychology* and *Division/Review*, journals of Division 39 (Psychoanalysis) of the American Psychological Association. He is Poetry Editor of *Division/Review*. He has been a member at large of the Board of Directors of Division 39 and its Publications Chair.

Table of Contents

Introduction... 1

I.   FROM AN ANALYST'S NOTEBOOK...................... 3

    Theological Countertransference 5
    Snapshots of the Psychotherapist Taken by Himself Without a
    Camera and Sometimes in Bad Light..................... 6
    From an Analyst's Notebook 12
    Tinnitus 16

II.   I ALWAYS DREAM OF SUBWAY TRAINS 17

    I Always Dream of Subway Trains 19
    Corn Soup... 20
    Snow Days 21
    The Story As I Understand It Is......................... 22
    Bubbameises... 24
    Good Rumor.. 25
    Kumquats 27
    Monty.. 28
    Unknown Soldiers..................................... 30
    Looking for Lola....................................... 32
    Turtle Story... 33
    Just Like Chicken 34
    Beggar's Chicken, Wellfleet, 1985 35
    Certain Death... 37
    What Is It About Water 38
    Acceptance Speech 39

III.   POEMS ON HOPPER PAINTINGS. 41
    Poems on Hopper Paintings. 43

IV. SPALDEEN. 47
    Spaldeen. 49
    Ars Poetica 50
    Writer's Block 51
    The Sweetness. 52
    Angelology 53
    Summer Body, Winter Mango 54
    Climate. 55
    Haircut 57
    The Heart Is Not The Red It Is Supposed To Be 59
    Grand Concourse. 61
    Double Sonnet for My Parents in which
    Xavier Cugat Makes a Guest Apearance 62
    Reincarnation 64
    Meditation on Love & Parrots 65
    Men Say Brown. 66

V.   LOST CHORD 69
    Pictures My Mother Left Me. 71
    Subway Suite. 75
    For a Friend Who Likes to Think His Dead Father
    Is Watching Over Him 79
    Lost Chord 81

Introduction

THESE POEMS, WRITTEN OVER several decades but never published as a collection, are a kind of autobiography—an account of concerns drawn from my life both inside and outside of my consulting room.

I'm a psychologist and psychoanalyst. My consulting room is a renovated garage, now an office and studio, next door to my house in Forest Hills, New York. It locates the adult consciousness that gives rise to my professional work and to these poems. My childhood home in New York's West Bronx locates the early consciousness and the developing consciousness that is (as for all of us) the ground for everything that follows in adulthood.

Hence the title. *"Spaldeen"* is what we called the ubiquitous pink rubber ball we played with, the name a corruption of the trademark "Spalding" which soon wore off or got covered with grime. The *spaldeen* was at the center of the physical, social, and much of the moral and psychological life of the kids who played on the streets and sidewalks of New York City—the emblem of a world.

As a psychotherapist and a poet, it's been my deepening experience that despite the obvious differences in aims, there's much alike in the two discourses. In each we try to discover language for making and shaping, for revealing, for pointing to, for formulating and for altering meaning. As I sit working in my office, the problem of getting the words right is much the same whether I'm trying to make sense of a patient's thoughts or of my own.

The Greek poet Yannis Ritsos said when a word is true "a meeting takes place." I hope something like that happens for a reader reading these poems.

May, 2016

I. FROM AN ANALYST'S NOTEBOOK

Theological Countertransference

I'm sitting on my consulting room floor playing War
with eight year old Jamie. He's here because he shits
in his pants when the nuns call on him in school
and I'm here to teach him to trust his mother's love
—and that it's no fault of his that his father's gone.
Both of us have our doubts. But we want to believe.
You Catholic? he asks me. I hesitate. Oh, he says
you're Public. There's something about this he likes.

But I remember when theology was not so easy.
Not in 1950 outside the library on Morris Avenue.
I've got my arms full of books and my little sister
in tow. We try to cross the street because I know
enough to know what's coming: Three 6th Graders
from *Saint Angela Merici's* eager to revenge
the death of Christ—on me—and the fact that I think
I had nothing to do with it cuts no ice with them.
Hey kid, you Jewish? No. You Protestant? No.
You ain't Catholic. I'm Agnostic, I say,
having already learned that only my mother
thinks Atheist is the right answer to anything.
But this is about history and blood and not
about believing. The inquisition's judgment
is inevitable. I'm pronounced full of shit
and I'm nailed: I'm Jewish. And I'm on my back,
the library books are in the gutter, my sister's crying,
and the angels have taken flight.

SNAPSHOTS OF THE PSYCHOTHERAPIST TAKEN BY
HIMSELF WITHOUT A CAMERA AND SOMETIMES IN
BAD LIGHT

Therapist, and teacher, years of this:
at times he wears a kind of chauffeur's cap.
He carries a small flag on a stick
the which he waves from time to time
so that the members of his party can find him
should they stray & leads his bunch
across the crowded floor of the Sistine chapel.
He points at God who points at Adam (who
wants to point at Eve or at the apple).
This, he explains, is how it all began....
They nod and think of lunch.

೩

Of course there's the sitting in the leather chair,
legs crossed, hand at the chin, the brain,
as it's getting late, a reluctant instrument
that only wants to watch a hockey game
or wonder what's for dinner. Still, it does it:
Attends, and, as if there were a knob for this,
fine tunes. And, again & once again,
he finds a voice and retells one or another
familiar, sad, particular and plaintive tale
with what he hopes is clarity & a modulated tone,
with the plot line, as for a child, simplified.
Which is to say, with hope in it.

೩

In his sleeveless undershirt and jockey shorts
he looks, he thinks, like the Chief Lifeguard—
gone a little fat but still tough enough
that the young ones give him the lifeguard salute.
Experience. You can tell he's pulled all kinds
out of the riptide, and more than once,
and one time, some things you can't forget,
it was this sweetiepie who in the struggle lost her top.
Dragged her up onto the beach, Heimliched her,
wiped the slime off with the inside of his wrist
and kneeling over her right there in the sand
gave her mouth to mouth. It never fazed him,
the silent watching faces, her bare cold tits.

❧

If he gets to heaven, if there is a heaven,
they'll be waiting for him in the reception hall
(he pictures the marble, the palm-filled atrium
in the New York Academy of Sciences);
they'll smile, take his coat, offer him a glass
of freshly squeezed tropical juice. He smiles
modestly. Modestly. As for the lives he saved:
there was no other way he could be or do.
He accepts another glass of juice.

❧

Falling asleep, he comes to various conclusions.
Here's one: All voyages take you home.
Years ago he read in Freud that discovery
is rediscovery, and years ago he thought
he understood—that what you find
is something you already knew, but more
than that: who you get to be is someone

you already are or were. Formulations
such as this yield to hypnagogic images
—usually sweet scenes. But then he dreams:
of his first car, which he owned in graduate school,
a 64 VW beetle, the color "anthracite",
the heat inadequate, but it chugged up
the snow-covered hilly streets in Washington Heights;
he wonders anxiously where it is now;
if it still starts.

☙

He thinks: inside of me there's a fat man
waiting to get out.... He thinks of the foods
he likes to think of even when his belly's full
(corn beef on rye, a sour pickle, Dr. Brown's Cel-Ray
which is what his father liked to drink, his Grandma's
rugalach). Sometimes after finishing lunch
he wishes he were hungry & could start again.
Homesickness, of course. But, strangely,
strange neighborhoods bring the symptoms on:
Chinatown, ethnic enclaves, ill-lit restaurants
where roast ducks drip in the windows
or plates of *chuchifritos* with exotic puddings
are displayed under signs he tries to read
but can't. He envies the other customers
who unfold foreign newspapers and order
in their native tongue, the laborers hunched
over bowls of pho. Spoon in the left hand,
chopsticks deftly in the right. The love songs
of another world playing in a loop.

☙

Sometimes he has time (say, an appointment
has been cancelled and it's a gloomy afternoon)
to try to improve his grip—and he reads a little
in the journals piled up & waiting on his desk.
"Sexual Sensations and the Gender Experience"
in one of last year's *Psychoanalytic Events*, for example,

where he finds an argument he can't quite follow
—which is psychoanalytic, but postmodern.
And post-structuralist, and post-deconstructionist.
And, post-feminist too—the author, a contemporary
Emily Post he thinks he met at a conference once.

But, as was said when modern meant the future
and not the past, he knows what he likes: The patient,
Miss M, would wrap herself tightly in her blanket—
to keep from coming apart—and touch herself "rigorously".
(So says Dr. Post and is allowed to by her editor
who may very well have read none of this.)
Well, he thinks: it makes the point! And he finishes
the article—a little more rigorous himself.

༄

He's been thinking about the sadness after sex,
about the loss, its cruelty and how it lasts
much longer than the finding just before it.

And of the stagey space, the silence, when
a magician makes a nearly naked lady disappear
(after the trick of sawing her and sawing her in half).

She had seemed, when he first conjured her,
so beautiful in her awkwardness as she climbed,
one white leg and then the other, out of the box

he had constructed out of nothing and
before your very eyes.

Then, with a lipstick smile, she climbs back in.

And then the show is over: that's all folks and
come again and don't forget to bring your friends.
And the theater lights are on, the traffic passes,
the birds will sing and the squirrels play squirrel
in the branches just outside the window.

೧

In the last hour before sleep he reads books
of exploration: solo journeys across Borneo,
in Amazonia, sailing single handed in the roaring 40s.

But his dreams are crowded—like the one
of being lost in a city where tree-lined boulevards
wind down to the harbor. Monumental plazas.
Statues of their heroes. Streetcars rumbling past.
He walks toward a destination he cannot specify—
or remember, or it changes. Those who live here
smile politely, and if they speak, offer distracted advice
on how to get to the place he tries to name.
Often he tries to make a phone call but he dials it wrong.
Or has attempted to write the number down,
say on a page of his spiral notebook
or on a scrap torn from the local newspaper.
But he cannot read what he has written.
Or he feels he knows the city but the neighborhood
is strange, crowded, dense with bodegas,
trattorias, delicatessens, the smell of frying,
sides of meat with fur still on, the heads of goats
hanging in the butchers' windows.

Then he's on the subway and trying to get home
—a home (he realizes this within the dream)
he hasn't lived in in a long long time. He changes
at a station which he thinks he recognizes
and waits among the others on the platform.

From an Analyst's Notebook

Case Report

I thought this would be a hard case:
a shell and only a little softer inside;
a walnut, maybe, the convoluted nut-meat
like two halves of a petrified brain.

I was no stranger to shells:
the egg you're careful not to crack,
the oyster which defies you to crack it,
the lobster you let cook in its own juice.

Then I saw: Oh, I said, an avocado
—leathery, then the soft soap, then
we would get to the impossible pit.

And there would be a ripening
like a mango, like a melon:
the sweetness a kind of dying really,
the way the mother dies
for the sake of the child.

Four O'Clock Hour,
Mozart on the radio in the waiting room

In the pauses one can hear the sound of the flute,
    through the closed door, diminished, but somehow pure.

The oboe is a cry baby; the operatic voice intrudes;
    the violin pleads its case but fails to move me.

The *tutti*s get obscured. But the flute comes through:
    a small ripple of inevitability, each note following

sweet & logical on the note that comes before—but more,
    the way a sentence is words but more than words.

And true, the way sighing is. Not a discovery
    a smaller thing, a rising, a reconciling.

Bird's Nest

The psychoanalytic third: *a term of art referring to the jointly created, unique, unconscious life of each analytic pair*

What about the nest the sparrows have built
between the separating boards
under the overhanging roof of my office?

What about the faint scratching?
Is the *psychoanalytic third* aware of the scratching,
of the vulnerability—

to the vicissitudes: the wind, a storm,
the neighbor's cat? Is the *third* troubled
by thoughts of the cat? Or by my intention

(as yet unarticulated) to call the roofer?
Or will it leave this to me
in my separate ambivalence?

What of the parenting, the feeding
of hatchlings? Our *third* must think
(however it thinks) about parents and hatchlings.

And the damage? Even to
my compassion. Damage *is,*
after all, what we're here about.

Ten AM., February

On the wall, over the Hans Hoffman poster,
in near-photographic reproduction and
by a trick of the morning sunlight reflected
off the windows of the house next door,
there are organic shadows: branches
of the rose-of-sharon planted against the fence
waving a little in a little breeze, film-like
shadows framed squarely by the shadow
of the winter-dusted window pane.
Last summer's last rose or the first roses
of the next—in the philosopher's cave.
That's the theory of this place: what we have framed
is the shadow of the form. The shadow of
the form of ancient love. And gloomy shadows
of ancient rage, sliding palely past us.
New memories of old things—if such a thing
is possible. The pain of remembered pain.
The discovered ache of absence. And forms of life:
intimations of a coming spring.

Tinnitus

A ringing, whistling, or other sensation of noise, which is purely subjective.
        —Webster's New Collegiate Dictionary, 1953

                    It's like a ringing in the ears,
a whistling, a kind of whisper —a sighing, a rising sound then
    falling,
like the ocean when you hear it in a seashell, except without the shell.
It's a murmur, a kind of gnawing. It's insistent like a hunger,
but receding like an echo, an echo that never quite fades to nothing.
I hear it in my sleep. I hear it now. It's a voice, but there are no words.
It's saying something or about to say something, but I can't say what
—maybe something someone on a Bronx street said
in another language, or I said it, or my father did, or it's a voice
on his table-top Philco radio coming from another room.
Or it's the sound between the words, like the static in the station
    break
or the sound of the crowd under and around the broadcast voices
when the Yankees played the A's, in Philadelphia, in 1948
and there were thunder storms between here and there. It's like a
    rumble
from somewhere in your chest, like exhaling changing to inhaling:
how the outbreath demands the inbreath demands the outbreath
    again
and that faint successive catching in the throat that is life succeeding
    life.
It's like a ringing in the ears....

II. I ALWAYS DREAM OF SUBWAY TRAINS

I Always Dream of Subway Trains

I'm on the Pelham line but you can't get to the West Bronx
from there. I've missed the change: the grimy corridor,
the vaulted ceiling, the iron bridge across the tracks.

The train—it's elevated now—is taking me away
past East Bronx tenements. I'll have to find a bus
or walk the half-familiar streets I used to know.

I always dream of subway trains. The wrong train:
The Broadway local; or I'm heading for South Ferry.
I know where I am, but I'm not going home.

And it's the way it always is: the feeling
that some act of will could take me home.
It's up to me to insist on this—

but if and when I do, things have changed.
The mail box is stuffed with uncollected mail.
The elevator won't come and then won't stop.

Grandma's still home, waiting for me. I'd forgotten.
And I just remembered. Or I tried to call and couldn't
get the number right. And time has passed.

And still I have this feeling that it's up to me.
And I think I can & I think I can't
& I think I can.

Corn Soup

A cold March night: the little Mexican place on 89th
where the strings of twinkling Christmas lights,
hand-cut doilies and red carnations on the tables
make one think of Christmas *and* of summer.
And the sad smiles of *las tres hermanas*
who run the place call to mind the three principles
of longing: dislocation, dislocation and dislocation.

I tell Sara, this corn soup takes me back
to the one my Grandma made, what, sixty,
more, years ago, and the way my father ate it:
hungry, in his undershirt and hunched over
the kitchen table in our apartment in the Bronx.
I mean with rye bead & butter, and if you take away
the beer & lime, the hot sauce, the taco chips....

Snow Days

I was an Eskimo—without all the words for snow,

no name for the melting kind but *melting*,
and then the sun comes out; no name for the sticking kind—
the kind you thought would last forever.

No name for a little snow in the air, then harder snow—
the kind that blows your breath away, that stings your face,
that fills your footprints even as you make them;

for what the snowplow piles on nights when otherwise
only the small song of snow-chains breaks the silence of the streets.

And there were nights I knew a snow day would be coming!
The sky glowed a kind of red, the light in my bedroom a kind of blue

—and everything was strange: the hour on the clock, the book
on my bedside table, my pile of cast-off clothes like a waiting animal.

The Story As I Understand It Is

I am an accident that happened on a trolley car.
I'm a chance meeting. I'm my father's shy recognition,
his awkward passage down the crowded aisle,
his introduction of himself and my mother's serious reply.
I'm a warmth rising in his chest and it won't cool down.
I'm her caution. I'm the way she notices
his surprising red hair, a thought interfering with her lesson plans.
I'm the trolley on a familiar track, the sparks jumping
from the overhead wire in the morning rain. I'm the rumble
of chance giving ground to something like intention.
I'm how he timed it after that so he'd be there at the trolley stop
when she was. I'm what they talked about that morning
and then the next. I'm the ring of the heavy black telephone
when he finally got his nerve up. I'm how they like
the first play they see together and how she still remembers
who was in it. I'm how he likes how serious she is,
how cleanly she speaks the language, what a mess
her desk drawers are. I'm how his hesitancy
reassures her; how his clumsiness makes her feel lovely.
I'm how they worry about money. I'm her passionate
social theories and his skeptical questions. I am how
she refuses to believe in God. And how he is not so sure.
I'm how something gets decided before anybody knows
that anything's been decided. And I'm the day it gets done:
the hotel wedding and the teachers' honeymoon cruise.
I am skin on skin and new pajamas, a new fan for the bedroom
humming in the shadows, lights from the curtained windows
sliding across the ceiling on an August night. I'm the bad news
from Europe and the outbreak of the War. I'm how
he almost went to fight, how his bag is packed,

and then he doesn't have to go: I'm that kind of luck,
that kind of comfort, the next morning (and the morning
after that), the sky through the bars of the fire escape
outside their bedroom window, the morning traffic
moving uptown and downtown, humming & fading
on the Concourse.

BUBBAMEISES
Yiddish: Old wives' tales; literally, Grandmothers' stories

Gottinieu!, my Grandma said and Aunt Bertie,
Aunt Bella & Aunt Annie would agree. And Mrs. Schaff
next door, and my sad Aunt Beatrice who came
to visit with shopping bags & candied orange peel
from *Barraccini's* and her own bittersweet *bubbameises.*
Their conversation at the kitchen table like the sound
of a soap opera on the Yiddish language station.

We managed to understand
what we managed to understand—
a word sometimes, a word in English, the import
of a silence, the music of an exclamation.
Go know! Grandma liked to say.
That we, *thank God,* are even here, alive
in the flicker of the *yahrzeit* lights lit for the dead,
and drinking tea and grateful—for the honey
of exaggeration, for the coarse salt of caution.
How beautiful they are (& spit three times),
these bright and milk-fed children we have left alive.

Good Rumor

                The way I heard them tell it
my father and my uncle peddled ice cream
uptown, in Washington Heights—at traffic lights
on Broadway and in the park off Riverside Drive
—so as to put themselves through college and
whatever else was in their lives in 33, and 4, and 5.

And at 4 o'clock with the summer sun still hot
and hanging in the sky across the Hudson,
ice cream was the field to be in. Sometimes,
in the humidity & haze, a kind of mania set in:
they'd call out, "Good Rumor, Good Rumor!",
slurring it a little out of the side of the mouth,
although there were no blue letters, no white box
—only the battered wooden one hanging heavily
from the shoulder on a strap.

                                I picture them,
look-alike brothers, one redheaded, one dark,
an eye out always for the cops, making change
from a changer at the belt, fingers burning from dry ice,
bringing a little unlicensed sweetness to citizens
in need of a taste of something else, some staring off
across the river stunned, some taking comfort
in the shade of Park Department elms or in the smoke
of a cheap cigar; others sprawled shirtless in the sun.

Later, in the 40's, I was there: my father and my uncle,
school teachers on a Saturday, pushing back
at the end of dinner from the heavy table

in our apartment in the Bronx, laughing the same laugh
from the same place in different throats. One or the other
sings out "Nice cold, ice cold...." An ice cream different
from the Breyer's brick their kids were spooning up.

We listened the way kids listen, heads bent
over our bowls, as if thinking of something else.
Like listening to the stories of stickball games
played once on an uphill street—
events in a long unsponsored Olympics
for the sons of immigrants—with consolation prizes
for finishing even if you didn't finish first.

Kumquats

Only Aunt Rita and Uncle Billy go to Florida. They fly
in an "airliner"—it's just after the War when we'd
still stop a street game to watch an airplane droning past
over the rooftops of the Bronx—because Uncle Billy
is an engineer who flew in Alaska during the War
and has rich parents who go for the winter to Miami Beach
where they visit at Christmas and send back a gift basket UPS,
a wooden crate of fruit packed in straw and citrus leaves:
grapefruits, oranges, and tangerines, and the spaces
between filled with kumquats which my father will peel
and eat raw—after the last grapefruit section
has been eaten and there's nothing left but the straw
and the bittersweet smell. He's holding a kumquat
and his mouth is puckering and he's in his undershirt
in the dining room, which after dinner is the bedroom
my sister shares with Grandma, and he's insisting:
This is *one of life's good things*. Oh Bernie, how can you
do that, my mother says. He turns to me, but I don't even
like them candied, which is what Grandma will do
with the last of them. *A real love affair*, Grandma is saying,
an engineer, the son of a rich man—retired, if you please,
a daughter playing golf in Florida and living, so help me,
like one of them now.

MONTY
1948

Monty always shook my hand. He kissed my little sister.
He had a black Buick Roadmaster, the grill of which grinned
like a mouth with chrome teeth.

He had a straw hat in summer and handpainted ties;
a sweet, insurance agent's drawl, a pack of Luckies
in one shirt pocket and a heavy hearing aid in the other.

He had an ex-wife in Alabama.
He had *Montague E. Foote* on his ID bracelet,
and a little *m*, big *F*, little *e* on his tiepin, and his cufflinks.

He took my schoolteacher Grandma to City Island and Atlantic
     City.
He knew fish houses downtown & how to eat a lobster.
He knew what to say—that the best thing to come out of the South
was the train going North.

But after they married, she complained to my mother:
he drank too much and his cough was waking her;
and his teeth came out at night and sometimes
he didn't come in until the next day. He took to sleeping
on the living room rug—for his back, he explained it;
and ate bananas & drank prune juice, finding harmony,
where he could get it.

He would sit in the window at the kitchen table, in the silence she
     left
when she left in the morning, in his undershirt,
with his Luckies and coffee and the *Daily Mirror*.

If I walked by that way on my way to school,
he might toss me a banana—to see if I could catch it.

And he bought me a bicycle. And a fishing pole.
And took me fishing once, now I remember it:
his hands shaking too much to bait the hook.

Unknown Soldiers

In an old joke a guy goes to the cemetery
to visit his father's grave. Nearby there is an unveiling.
The stone reads: *Saul Bernstein, Unknown Soldier.*
He asks an old man among the mourners
please to explain. As a *soldier*, he was unknown,
the man says —but was he a furrier!

I think of Papa Irving in his overalls
running the freight elevator at his factory. He's talking—
about his daughter the principal, his daughter
the head librarian, his son the professor, his son-in-law....
Irv, says a customer, as they jerk to a stop on Three,
you're overqualified.

Uncle Lou could make a nickel disappear
in his cigar stained fingers & find it again in my ear.
Uncle Norman, when he was happy, hummed *con brio*
and would accompany himself with little farting noises
made with the hands clasped as if in prayer.
Uncle Bubby lost his leg & got a wooden leg & walked
like the crazy man he was. My Russian Uncle, Nat,
was the unknown furrier—but was he a philosopher!
What is it to eat?, he would ask—after dinner.
What is it to be a Jew? He would insist I answer.
What is God? What is goodness? What is it to know?

My father, dead now half my lifetime—should I say unknown
in his?—now *he* was a teacher. He would recall his first class,
1932, September, James Monroe High School in the Bronx:
How he removes his grandfather's gold pocket watch

from the vest of his own blue suit. He winds it and
places it carefully on the desk. Afterwards he collects
his books & papers, and, Oh God, he sees the watch is gone.
How he never recovers the watch—or forgets the lesson.
Or lets me forget it: How you learn to learn
from what you lose.

Looking for Lola

If there's something dark in this morning's sunlight,
there is an English word for it. But as Doctora Ramirez y Castilla
my second year Spanish professor explained wistfully:
there is no good word for *mood* in Spanish.
I sat near skinny Vivian who never said a word
in Spanish—or in English—and didn't look like much
until I saw her one night in the *Thespians'* "Damn Yankees".
She was Lola—Lola tango, red rose Lola—breasts,
body, hips and she could get whatever she wanted
and, little man that I was, I wished she wanted me.
Let me put it this way, it changed the mood in Spanish Two.
I kept looking sideways at Vivian that whole Spring,
looking for Lola. Not that that was just a mood. It lasted longer,
like longing—for which there has to be a Spanish word.
Mood is less than longing and you could say darker,
like a shadow, a cloud, like the shadow of a cloud.
There's always a kind of darkness there. I don't know why
the Spanish can't say that.

Turtle Story

                    Once we sent Josh home
from the Burns Street park for a strawberry.
We gave him the key, he was that kind of kid,
he was four, and ran all the way and then back
with a berry as big as his fist—for the snapping turtle
which Bobby Hussian had just come back with
from visiting his father in the country. Bobby'd said,
It eats *strawberries*. We doubted that. We gathered
in a circle, parents & children in the fading summer light
—I think the light was fading but that may be the romantic
in me. Did I say it was a Sunday afternoon in June?
The turtle was refusing to come out, an imitation of a coffin
the size of a grown man's hand. You have to see
the scene—the park, the light, the circle of parents
and children, the turtle on the grass, the strawberry placed
in front of it, the red, the green. The turtle stirs a little,
extends its head. This is the first we've seen it has a head.
It takes a turtle-step toward the strawberry, graceful
in a way, smoother than you might think from anything
you think you know of turtles. It takes a bite! Another bite!
It is voracious. Can you say that about turtles?
It was a kind of miracle. The turtle ate the strawberry!
Have you ever heard a story where everyone
lived happily ever after—and you believed it?
It was something like that.

Just Like Chicken

One hot and humid night, in the early 60s, in July,
my Grandma Foote served me and Sara,
my eagerly polite & newly wedded wife,
her long-promised *specialité*, frogs legs deep fried.

Because I was her boy, the one who loved
what she loved to cook, which in this case
looked like a pile of blackened elbows
on a platter on her crocheted table cloth.

And would taste, she assured us *just like chicken*.

Which these did—a little, which meant they didn't.
And when we wouldn't—couldn't—manage seconds,
there was a strangling silence at the heavy table—
long after the long strange bones were in the trash

and all through the peach cobbler & vanilla ice cream
that followed for dessert. Only the electric fan
humming on the sideboard and through the open window
the sounds of the street. Oh, unrequited love: it hurts.

Beggar's Chicken, Wellfleet, 1985
~ *for Richard and Joan Zuckerberg*

I remember the summer parties,
the wine in paper cups,

the time we made
Beggar's Chicken.

We dug a pit in the sand,
lined it with stones, built a fire over it.

There would have been laughing, jokes—
probably about stuffing the chicken.

We dug it up—and ate it
with our fingers.

Afterwards we went down a winding path
to the ocean, stripped off our clothes

left them at the foot of the dune,
swam naked in the dark.

Like remembering & remembering again
an old movie, one we loved.

We can name the actors who were in it
—even those no longer making pictures.

Beggar's Chicken is a Chinese banquet dish attributed in legend to a beggar who steals a chicken and then in fear of being caught buries it and builds a fire over it. When later he digs it up and breaks open the brick of clay that has formed around it, the chicken is roasted to perfection. These days the bird is stuffed with rice and savories and wrapped in lotus leaves before the mud goes on. When it's served, the baked brick is opened with a hammer & chisel at table, a treasure-in-a-rock worthy of an emperor.

Certain Death

I'm the three doomed Jews in the terrorist joke:
the one who loves his life; the one who preaches;
the one who pleads, shoot me *before* the sermon.
I'm the inspector who missed the pistol
in the duffel bag; the pilot going God-knows-where;
the smiling flight attendant whose poor children play
in some part of this indifferent world, while a jealous lover
waits in another. I'm the reporter with a notebook standing
on the tarmac; the flight controller in the tower, pretending
to make order. I've got too much to say in the time
that's left to me to say it in. And I've heard it all before.
The rumors of my death have been exaggerated,

but they're also understated. My story's on page one
& continued in the theater section; my obituary filed
while facts are being gathered. My achievements
speak for themselves, but in a hoarse stage whisper.
My funeral will be a quiet one and dignified; my ashes
left to be disposed of by those who loved me best:
scattered in the rubble, dusting the construction site,
the cinders rising in a rising wind, entering the rain,
mixing in the mortar—like ash from an extinct volcano,
giving strength to the footings, to the viaduct, even
to the cistern. I'll be the rain and what collects the rain—
water for my children's children.

What Is It About Water

that we're always comparing it to other water?
Like the last tide; or how yesterday, it seems,
the waves were rougher; or what we swam in
on another coast. Or carried up in buckets
to build castles with. Or the pond I swam in
as a child and my father thought Lake George
was colder. Or the way it was, my father said, when
his father tossed him into the surf at Rockaway.

Once, in the sand at Coney Island, I found
a pocket watch, inscribed *To Monseigneur F....*
I looked him up. And brought it back to him.
He told me he's retired now and time is on his hands
and he takes the D train from Midtown out to Coney—
which takes him back: to the Danube before the War
& diving for the coins that tourists tossed to naked boys
and that, he says, was water!

                                      My own father's
gold standard was Jones Beach. You had to drive
an hour out from the Bronx to get there—which we did
when I was ten in a '49 Nash Ambassador. The uplift!
The difference from the Rockaway that he remembered!

And as for Longnook Beach in Truro: Yes, he said, yes
beautiful—how the sand cliffs slope down to the sea,
and, yes, the clarity. The two of us are floating on our backs
beyond the line of breakers. He turns and does a stroke
or two of his sweet & measured crawl. Like Jones! he calls,
from a little distance now, except the waves were bigger!

Acceptance Speech

And I want to thank the women—my teachers, my editors, certain professors, even the course assistants, but first my mother, who taught me the principles of right and of grammar as if they were nursery rhymes and recited me my nursery rhymes as if they were principles. And I want to say thank you to the blue haired teachers at PS 35, Bronx who taught us penmanship, headings, margins, silence, the uses of convention, and the value of dread. And particularly Miss Girdis, who taught me long division—so I would know what patience can accomplish and how even the right answer can be endlessly a mess. I want to express my gratitude to my Grandma who taught me addition without subtraction: that you can love one and, equally, more than one—and to my other Grandma who taught me that even the old miss their mother. I want to thank my sister whom I once called a "little rat", and for which I am sorry, because from her and by her I learned unreason and the power of whim—but also taking turns. I want to extend my heartfelt thanks to the women who picked me to squander their attentions on. And I want to say thank you, yet again, to my wife—the bright lady of my sonnets. But, honestly, thanks to the dark ladies, too, starting with the cousin I had a crush on before I knew it was a crush, and the aunt, the first of many I had a crush on after I knew it was a crush. I want to thank women for the bureau drawers I could hardly pull open when I was three, and for the smell of talcum and eau de cologne. For the garter belts, the mysteries. For the way my aunts' conversation stopped when I blundered into it. I want to thank the girls in public school—who lined up on the other line, came in sometimes through the other door, whose hands were always in the air & confident, who colored prettily and kept within the lines. I want to thank them all for seventh grade, for that way they had of carrying their books wrapped in their arms against their breasts. For high school, for their skating sweaters, for college seminars, the hair pinned back, the chewing on a pencil, for teaching me to kiss with an open mouth. And I want to thank the dreamers, the dark ones, the bright ones, and the teachers of dreaming who live mostly in the dark. I thank them, even for my bad dreams, even for the dreams I may never understand.

III. POEMS ON HOPPER PAINTINGS

Poems on Hopper Paintings

"Corn Hill, Truro, Cape Cod, 1930"

Late summer. This is how the world was once
and what the world will be when we have left it,
what the sun will shine on, the light still warm—
the world growing cold, the weathered cottages
like mausoleums of summers past, when children
carried pails & shovels down to the beach and
in the evenings played hide and seek; then, called in
to sleep, their voices in the shadows pleading
for a few more moments of this sweet this,
almost indistinguishable from the sound
of the crickets in the dune grass.

"Rooms for Tourists, 1945"

Provincetown, evening, a summer night.
An old white house, newly painted for the season,
asserts itself—as if the house & sign, saying *Rooms*,
were an argument: as if electric light could argue
with the enormous black. The promise argues
with the loneliness and almost has a voice.
On the radio, you think, a saxophone: Soon, soon
a tourist in a striped boat-shirt will leave the parlor
to the brief percussive slam of a warped screen door.
A moonless sky, but luminous, absorbs the light.
You think: There's something behind all this—
a larger argument that one is bound to lose.
Beyond the street, the pine forest and the dunes;
beyond the dunes, the ocean argues with the shore.

"Drug Store, 1927"

                Light itself is the prescription,
at once a stimulant and soothing. The drug store
is empty at this late hour, except, you imagine,
for a worried husband waiting on a bent-wood chair.
The tiled floor is washed & smells medicinal.
The druggist, practiced in the mysteries, counts out pills.
The girl behind the counter at the soda fountain
turns the pages of a penny tabloid which promises
to reveal various and lurid details....

The light says this is a matter of life and death.
It says: Here is a tonic. The light cuts through
as though there were no inside and our smallest ills
were public. The alchemy of Ex-Lax is offered,
blue and stenciled on the window.

"Eleven am, 1926"

She is nude, in shoes, sitting at the open window.
The sun is hot; her skin is cool. This is a mid-town hotel
for one-night husbands. There is a need for air.
The heavy curtains are drawn back. She has nothing
left to hide; still, even now, even here, she hides.

What she doesn't know is why the possibility excites
her, why she could just go out that window and hit—
dying, there, on that sidewalk, naked as she is, and
moaning, beautiful, bloody, legs apart & cunt
an open wound, and stared at by every goddamn
salesman in a hat.

"Sunday, 1926"

The storefront windows are empty
or are shaded—like eyes of the dead.
The sun lights an empty street. All the shade,
and all the shadows, are inside.

He sits alone on the wooden stoop
and small—as if in the gaze of witnesses
who are mute, or yawning and indifferent.
He's left his worn suit jacket with nothing
in the pockets in an upstairs room,
leaving that silence to sit in this one.

He holds himself. He has only
the strength in his shoulders, and his considering.
There is nothing and no one else to hold.

"Room in New York, 1932"

                      A crisis.
The kind of waiting that is forced upon us:

a front room where, bright as it is, the light is
never bright enough to see things clearly by,
where the time is marked by the idle sound
of an out of tune piano, which suffices.

This note is a love note, she says, or could be.
And this is how what is wounded in him
goes to hide, in the half read pages
of the morning paper, under the white shirt
and tie. Not that he thinks that.

Poems on Hopper Paintings

He keeps his mind on politics. Something
he can get a grip on: He is thick in the wrist
and forearm and has his sleeves turned up.

"Approaching a City, 1946"

You are about to go down into a blackness,
a hole in the light, along with the train
that disappears into the tunnel to the City.
Park Avenue, the Bronx, 1946, the long tunnel
to Grand Central, the all-day train ride
back from the Adirondacks at the end of summer.
My sister and I told and retold moron jokes
although she was four and didn't get them:
*Why did the moron bring bread & butter
to 42nd Street? He wanted to eat the traffic jam.
Why did the moron throw his watch out the window?
He wanted to see time fly.* Of course Hopper
isn't interested in time passing—he's painted
the idea of approach, not the progress.
He omits the obvious foreshadowing details:
cinders in the air, the massing of electric wires,
the thickening, black & incomprehensible disorder.
Now, a dizzying switch from day to night
is about to happen—which on the train
will come suddenly like a slap
from an exhausted and impatient parent,
inevitable, but still stunning. There will be a roaring
as if the blackness had a voice.
And a learning—something harsh, something
you didn't want to know.

IV. SPALDEEN

Spaldeen
1957, CCNY

Imagine a rubber ball, says our World History professor
who is explaining the "great circle" route,
the shortest distance from the Old World to the New,
a thing sons of immigrants can well imagine
from the street games we all grew up on: *Stickball,
Boxball, Chinese Handball, Off the Point....*

On a sphere—he's pointing at an invisible globe
held in his left hand—a straight line is always polar....

But I can only see smudged continents, a darkness
that might be Europe. I can only think of going West
and of my grandfather, born in Poland but never Polish,
a boy getting off a boat—and of the line described
by a journey on the IRT from the Lower East Side
to the West Bronx and the Grand Concourse,
of the end of the War, of Feldmann's candy store,
the penny candies and the wire bin of *spaldeens*
new & pink & powdered and one of them,
if I could only get a quarter from my father,
waiting to be mine.

Ars Poetica

One cluttered room opens on another:
Even your bedroom closet leads somewhere.
Behind the clothes in mothballs, at the back, behind the cartons
filled with only your mother knows what, there's a trapdoor
leading to a passage which leads to other rooms,
rooms in your own house you never knew were there,
rooms furnished oddly: wicker where you have walnut,
white where yours are dark, the paintings are not the kind
your mother hangs. There's a half strung harp; ferns in ceramic pots.
There's a parrot singing sailor songs and cursing and shocking the
    ladies.
Still, it's your own relatives who live there—lost cousins,
the uncle who never returned from the Amazon.
Probably it's his parrot. His common-law Brazilian wife
cooks black beans on a blackened stove. He's made millions
and lost millions trading on the river. He offers you
some trinkets, carved and beaded, and possibly of value
to bring back with you if you want to.

Writer's Block

I heard it on the radio: this odd Brazilian fish
that eats nuts and fruits. *Nuts and fruits?*
the interviewer asks. Yes. The Amazon floods
the surrounding jungle. The fish swims into the jungle
and eats what's there on the forest floor, berries
in particular—making its flesh especially sweet,
(in the opinion of the interviewee). When the water
recedes, the fish goes back into the muddy river.
And no one said what it lives on between floods.

The Sweetness

A Zen master is chased by a tiger to the edge of a precipice. He stumbles and is caught on a thorny branch. He hangs over the abyss. Above him, the tiger. Growing there next to him, wild strawberries. He reaches out and plucks one. How delicious! he giggles.

I've picked wild strawberries
with my little sister, at the edge of the woods
behind a rented cottage, in Old Forge, New York,
strawberries the size of a baby's thumbnail
and sweeter than the tiny carrots we pulled
from other people's gardens, and sweeter
than the apples we shook from someone's tree
and better than the stalks of ripening rhubarb
we stole and chewed raw.

One July Sunday I ate seventeen popsicles.
All afternoon Davey Wallace and I got sodas
for the players in the American Legion baseball game.
Each 2 cents back was ours—for popsicles:
cherry and grape and orange and lime; colors,
not flavors exactly, but icy—and delicious.

Maybe we knew there would be consequences:
stomach aches, stains, we'd get home late,
our activities insufficiently explained....
But what I remember is the sweetness;
and the wild, drunken, thirst for more of it;
and the feeling: what it feels like to be rich.

Angelology

How many angels can dance on the head of a pin?
It all depends: On the pin, on which angels,
on the space they're willing to give
each other to be an angel in.

On the spread of their wings.
Even to themselves, angels are a mystery:
different beings, strange bedfellows....
What is it you expect of me?

a shining one might whisper, lips to her partner's ear,
slow dancing on the tiny dance floor.
What are my choices? He might whisper
back. Or, *Expect? Jesus! Just shimmer!*

At which there's a sensation of falling, a silence
(that seems to last an eternity) and the music dies.

SUMMER BODY, WINTER MANGO
For Ozzie Siegel

It's been a summer for good weather
and bad news. I'm sitting on the beach
thinking about my friend Ozzie
who said from his hospital bed: if it ends
in an *o m a*, you don't want it.
But he'd got it. The blue sky
is exceptionally blue. The waves
rise like possible thoughts.
A little plane flies just offshore
trailing a banner advertising suntan lotion.
I think: How about a message
worth squinting into the sun for?
How It All Depends On The Body.

☙

The day after Ozzie's funeral
I saw an old man considering a mango.
It was under the awning of the *Fruit & Vegetable*.
The rain was washing the blizzard away.
A grapefruit and he could have been my father—
the way he considered. He could be remembering
his first mango, I thought, and maybe an island,
and maybe a woman, I thought romantically,
the smell of the rain would help with that.
These were a dollar forty-nine but
no sure thing. Another of those chances.
They pile up like that. They are uncountable,
which doesn't make them infinite.

CLIMATE

Karma, explains my sweet son Dan,
is: "The way you treat people, that's how
they'll treat you—even if they're other people"
which states the faith: that there's a disorderly
moral order, maybe invisible, but as real
as the one by which the flight of a butterfly
in a tropical rain forest causes, unpredictably,
a snowstorm in the Northeast corridor and
because the schools are closed that day—
college, I should say, I'm thinking of 1959
when his mother and I were kids ourselves
(and only starting on our way to causing him)
and went to schools on adjacent city hills,
hers to the south and mine north of 125th Street,
with a great social gulf between them I should add
but the same "snow day" for both, and in a blizzard
we walked to *Addie Vallins* for hot chocolate
and then back to my family's five room place
on the Grand Concourse in the Bronx,
one room of which was mine for making out in,
which we did when we should have been
studying my Spanish and her Chem,
and I never got past page one of the lesson
on certain irregular conjugations, which page
when I turned to it later in Doctora Ramirez's class
(the snow by then having melted and refrozen
and random icy patches decorated the sidewalks
and the city had returned to its winter gray)
gave off a heat which distracted me and
I had no good answer for the Professora, yet again.

But I thank her because there was a softness there,
—or it was the *climate*: Instead of failing me,
she let me pass.

HAIRCUT

I step out of *Spectrym* hair salon in Forest Hills
disguised as one of my neighbors, blown dry,
smelling of Georgina's talcum, itching and remembering
the *Italian Brothers Barbershop* on 161st Street
in the Bronx and the way the clippers left prickly hair
at the back of my neck & down my back and smelling
of Vitalas rubbed in and drying to a crust on the wave
I would have asked Antonio for the comb to do myself.

He smiles professionally and asks if I'm "Ba' Mitz" yet
and doesn't believe me when I say no but I don't say
it's because we're Atheists and I'll never be "Ba' Mitz".

All he knows is I'm not Catholic, so I must be Jewish
(this is the Bronx, its 1953, and those are the choices)
and I have sideburns already which need the attention
of the straight edged razor; and at thirteen I should pay
full price. He whacks the razor on his leather strop
and thinks he's being tricked.

                    And I remember
hot Septembers when I played tennis with my father
on Rosh Hashanah when everyone we knew &
everyone we didn't know was dressed for the Holidays.
We wore shorts and walked the long way to the courts
to avoid the synagogue. I carried the racquets, since,
he explained, I was only a kid, which didn't make
much sense to me even then

                    but now I know he had
enough to carry—being the grandson of the rabbi
I had only seen in formal photographs: European suit
and hat and white beard spreading across his chest.

And I step out into sunlight onto Austin Street
carrying myself like anybody's next door neighbor,
a citizen with nothing on his mind but hair.

THE HEART IS NOT THE RED IT IS SUPPOSED TO BE
1945, The Bronx

My white-haired grandmother remembers her own red hair.
She pushes an empty baby carriage.
Her legs are bowed. She is *no sixteen years old no more.*
She is not twenty-three —when her first baby, David,
died of diphtheria.
Her black cloth coat is pinned at the neck with a safety pin.
She leads us (my sister and me) over the iron bridge over the tracks
and the wires of the train yard.

There is the sweatsmell of the blacksmith's—
shoeing the last of the last of the fruit peddler's horses;
the chicken market sound of the chickens and the smell
of the shit of the chickens

—and the eye & the beak of the chicken.
The butcher laughs; he lifts his knife; he cuts off the head.
The wings beat as it gives up its blood.
It struggles in his hand, although it is dead.
There is blood on the sawdust, blood on his apron;
the smell of feathers burning.

Grandma sits on a stepstool at the kitchen sink.
She is braced against the sink.
She will pluck the pin feathers.
She will plunge her hand to the wrist in filth.
She will pull out the *kishkes*. The guts are yellow.
The liver is purple and slippery. The feet are terrifying.
She will tease me with the terrible feet.
The heart is not the red it is supposed to be.

She will fry up the heart in a frying pan,
she will fry the liver, she will fry the gizzard,
this for a child of her heart.
Tender, she salts my food for me. I will forgive her.
I will tear the center from the slice
of the *kimmel* bread she gives me.
I will eat the heart at the kitchen table.
Still my feet do not reach the floor.
I will chew it. It is the size of a mother's nipple.
It is the size of half of my thumb.
It is tougher.

GRAND CONCOURSE
early 1940s

Quasi-photographic images
cast by the headlights of passing cars:
of the windows, of the individual panes,
of the curtains, of the window guards—
oddly angled rectangles of light
slide through each other
and over the ceiling & the walls all night,
disembodied *presences*, populating my room.

I can see any three spots on the wall
as faces—two eyes and the nose
of animals come from fairy tales.
And then, despite my mother's visits,
her *just one more* kisses, I lie in bed,
blanket to my chin and still.

Double Sonnet for My Parents in which Xavier Cugat Makes a Guest Apearance
The Bronx, 1950

The Victrola was in the hallway
in a cabinet with red leatherette doors
and slots for storing the albums they
thought we should be listening to.

The automatic changer would click,
& a record would drop. You had to turn the stack
halfway though The Nutcracker,
the Strauss Waltzes, Beethoven's Fifth.

But there *were* pop singles for the mambo,
the rhumba, for the fox trot and the tango,
for the lessons they'd signed up for
at Arthur Murray's up on Fordham Road.

Oh, they *started out to go to Cuba*. Box step—
but carefully so the needle wouldn't skip.

It was like painting by numbers
as might be applied to dancing the rhumba.
Daylight between them—deliberate,
so as not to step on each other's feet.

Daddy in his undershirt, Mother serious—
attending to the sequence, the lesson.
What their dreams were I can only imagine.
They never went "out"—except to the movies

which was the way *romantic* came to The Bronx:
uptown by bus to The Loew's Paradise,
or downtown by subway to Radio City.
The Ed Sullivan Show on black & white TV.

But there on the Grand Concourse, 4th floor, *Oh,*
palm trees were whispering yo te quiero....

Reincarnation
for Sara

After we made love today I thought:
I must have been a good dog in my last life.
Good dogs just jump into the ocean
& bring you back a stick & bring it back again.
They stay, they come, they sleep at your feet,
they wait patiently while you run your errands.
I thought: I must have saved a drowning kid,
or been the one who warns the people,
or finds his way home again
from another country and nobody knows how
he got across the water. It's simple really,
he got across the water because he loves you.
Today, after we made love, I thought:
That would explain it—this life is the reward!
A body *and* a mind. And the mind at home
in the body, and the body the best friend
a mind could ever dream of, the salt
on its tongue, and the wet muzzle and
the whole animal smell of it.

Meditation on Love & Parrots

So a woman in a mink walks into a pet shop
and she's thinking of a parrot.
Have I got a bird for you! the owner says,
Pull his left leg, he sings God Bless America.
Pull the right: I'm A Yankee Doodle Dandy.
And what, she wants to know, if I pull both legs?
At this the parrot opens up an eye:
Missus! he croaks, You wanted a singer or a dancer?

You know who told that joke? My father-in-law.
He could do a perfect Yiddish accent.
And you know who always laughed? My mother-in-law.
I think he wanted to be everything for her—
which is what she wanted, too.
They knew it was impossible, may they rest in peace,
which is why he told the joke, and why she laughed.

Men Say Brown

On the radio this morning: The average woman knows
275 colors—and men know eight. Women say coffee,
mocha, copper, cinnamon, *taupe*. Men say brown.

Women know an Amazon of colors I might have said
were green, an Antarctica of whites, oceans of colors
I'd stupidly call blue, fields of color, with flowers in them
I would have said were red.

From women, I've learned to love the browns,
the earths, the dusts, the clays, the soft colors, the colors
brought out from the mines, hardened ones,
hardened in fires I would call red; the colors of the furies;
the reconciling colors of the cooling ash.

By myself I know the evening colors when the sky goes
from blue to another blue to black—although it's a lonely,
whitish black sometimes,

                    like the color of sleep—
the way dreams are lit by the light that's thrown
from nowhere on the things you find in them. Last night
there was a turtle, I would say it was brown or green,
or it was a snake, mottled, a kind of grey, disguised
as a turtle, red spots as if painted on the shell,
a palish greenish underside—vulnerable, alone
swimming in water I would say was colorless.

I woke to the pale colors of the morning—no one
has a name for those: the white-rose white you see
through the white of the curtains on the window,
the milks, the creams, the cream a galactic swirl
before it turns to brown when your wife stirs it in the coffee,
the faint drying oval on the silver of the spoon.

V. LOST CHORD

Pictures My Mother Left Me

Rockaway Beach, March

My father is at the center of my mother's picture—his rough collar turned up against the wind, looking out to sea. In the distance there is a stone breakwater. The sea is gray, as is the sky and the sand. Different grays. My father is in his sixties (younger than I am now), his red hair faded and cut too short; his neck and shoulders muscular. He might be a retired stevedore, or a sailor. But the image is misleading. Still, my mother likes it, likes to think of him this way—although she knows that my father is not a man of action. Neither is he a man of thought (I mean accomplished thought), but he does seem to be thinking now. He's not so much looking at the sea as looking at *something* by looking at the sea. What that is she doesn't know and neither, probably, could he say. But my mother understands my father's inwardness-disguised-as-outwardness because this is the way she looks at things herself. I'm the child of dreamers.

Hadrian's Wall

In her fading color photograph, Hadrian's Wall is a narrowing road, an ancient footpath along the top of what's left of a rocky embankment winding across a gray-green heath and vanishing in a cloudy North of England sky. As a wall, it's keeping no one from anything—although for centuries it marked a divide between a here which was known and a there which terrified. As a road, it leads where it seems to lead: nowhere. The few idle tourists in the picture (in the distance, atop the wall) seem by their unhurried pointing and picture-taking postures to take this for granted. My father is there in the lower left hand foreground and probably in this picture only by photographic accident. This was just a year before he died. You do not see his face. His back is to the camera. I'd guess he'd be a little bored and, characteristically, a little restless. An end is approaching but how could he know that? And how can my mother know, absorbed as she is with the viewfinder, the perspective, the vanishing point?

Tintern Abbey

These lines were composed by my mother and not by Wordsworth—the dark against the light, a jagged stone arch silhouetted against a milk-white sky. She enjoys framing the irony—walls meant to house an Eternal Spirit eternally gradually demolished by the slow wrecking ball of history. She knows the long story, she could tell you: the Black Death of 1354, the abolition of the monasteries, the romantic pretensions of the Nineteenth Century, the restorers of the Twentieth.

Although she tries to wait until there are none, other tourists, singly and in twos, occupy the center of her picture, momentary, tiny, and in tension with the larger looming mystery of the ancient walls. Their presence in the view-finder disturbs my mother, upsets her platonism—like unwanted thoughts. Random instances of miscellaneous color in the "bare ruined choir". A woman in a kerchief and a red raincoat; a man with his hand on his chin, considering. She knows my father is there too—outside the frame, waiting for her.

Corrida (Bullfight), rural Peru

A small crowd of spectators is seated on an embankment in the ancient ruins, the men, the women both in felt brimmed hats. They are locals, *indios*, small and brown, the children smaller versions of their parents. My mother likes the scene, likes the mountain wall rising behind them, appreciates the history—these are descendants of the Incas who staged & watched their own sanguinary games in this valley, survivors of the conquistadors who left them bullfights among other agonies. But there are things my mother cannot bear. She turns her camera away from the doomed bull, the cheap pageant. She studies the spectators, their casual possession of the old stones; their bundles tied in scarves; their heads in profile pointed in the same direction—like the crowd at a tennis match, but solemn and their rooting interest is unknown. If you look closely, there in the crowd, seated among people too shy to speak to him even if he speaks in Spanish (which in any case is not their language either), there is a bearded *gringo*. A young man with long hair. I don't think my mother sees him; I don't think he sees her. 1973. I wore my hair like that when I was thirty-three.

Robinson Crusoe

"Robinson Crusoe" she would say, with a dismissive laugh, of this faded early 70's photograph of me, wanting me and everyone to know she didn't care for the wild hair & beard and faded tee shirt—although the beard was a familiar mahogany, the color of my father's hair. But all her life she kept *this* face in a crystal frame on the bookcase in her foyer where it would be the first thing that when I or anyone came to see her we would see. And it was she who read Robinson Crusoe to me, as a bedtime story, tenderly, before I could read it for myself.

Lake Louise

Lake Louise, with Ida is what she scrawled (years later) across the back. They shared a double room at the rustic lodge—because it was cheaper and they'd be less alone now that there were no husbands in the picture—and hiked with their lunch and cameras and sensible shoes to this point above the tree line.

It's cold here, although it is summer. The glacier winds away to the north. The Canadian Rockies rise sharply above the still, pale, turquoise water—the water a blue unlike any blue she's ever seen. The upthrust layers of rock are reflected in the lake; the composition is perfect. No people. No Mack, no Bernie to hurry them along. The evergreens below bring to mind the fur of the short-haired terrier that ran away from home when she was a child.

Ida is not in the picture but is in my mother's idea of the picture. Louise, one of Queen Victoria's mostly forgotten daughters, is in her idea too. I imagine they talked about their own children—not on the walk back down, but often enough. And they talked about their husbands, a little, at dinner when they considered the menu—missing them but missing them a little less by now: how Bernie never liked fish because of the bones and how tonight she thinks she'll have the trout.

Subway Suite

Blue Ball

E train to Manhattan. In the next section of seats facing me and forward of me is a child who looks to be about two or three sitting on his mother's lap. He is speaking in a loud complaining voice in a language I do not understand and squirming restlessly while she tries to quiet him. His voice above the sound of the train is the only human sound in the subway car.

The train stops at Queens Plaza, their stop. As they are getting up, there's a single loud click—but I don't see what might have caused it. The boy is protesting as his mother hustles him off the train, her shopping bags in one hand, his wrist in the other. The doors shut. The train lurches forward out of the station. I look back down to the page of my magazine, to the poem I've been trying to make some sense of. As I do, I catch a glimpse of something coming down the aisle. It's a small blue ball, propelled backwards by the acceleration of the train. It rolls past the white pole, straight down the center of the car. On impulse I extend my leg and catch it with my foot. A blue wooden ball! That's what the kid was upset about! He had dropped this. I hold it a moment under my foot. One or two people seem to notice, but they keep their noticing to themselves, hardly looking up from their newspapers (many of those in foreign print), hardly interrupting their own thoughts. I exchange glances with the pretty, dark-skinned young woman sitting diagonally to my left. I offer a minimal smile; she doesn't smile back. I'm on my own with this. I release the ball. It starts to roll again—and rolls away behind me through the half-empty car. It disappears.

Violin

On the platform at 53rd and Lexington a small man is bending over a violin case that he has put down on the platform. The case is an elaborate one with compartments for bows, rosin, strings—the kind you'd want for taking a violin on a long voyage. His violin looks worn and the finish is dull—but as he tunes it up it is apparent that this is a good one. The man looks to be Chinese and he is not young. This is clearly a routine: He sets up, his back against a pillar, the open case in front of him, a coin or two already in it. An E train headed the other way roars into the station, the doors open, slam closed; the train pulls out. In the relative silence that follows, the man begins to play—something classical, arpeggiated, obviously something he has played so many times the edges have been polished off. The notes slide one into the next. The station is filling, it's just before rush hour. The platform is full of city high school kids carrying their books, talking loudly, shouting to each other. The only quiet ones are wearing earphones.

I feel a kind of fright for him—I think it's fright, I think for him—for how odd, alien, and vulnerable he is: the music of the Eighteenth Century, of the European courts, on a fragile instrument of Italian Renaissance design; the filthy platform, the jostling high school kids, the others who hardly give him even a curious glance much less listen, much less listen appreciatively or generously. But the man himself is calm, impassive: no clues as to what he might be thinking or, of course, what language he might be thinking in. And for all I can tell this is better than what he's come from—maybe a political prison or other starvations or humiliations.

Now he plays his version of Fur Elise, a piece I played a long time ago when I was a kid in the Bronx, when I was taking piano lessons from Mrs. Rothstein down the block. My parents thought music lessons would be a good for me and the Rothsteins were refugees from Europe and needed the money.

Bagpipe

Another day there is a bagpipe player on the same platform: 53rd and Lexington. Now the station is filled with bagpipe music. The player is not wearing a kilt: He's a tall blond guy in trousers—red-faced from puffing and squeezing. People glance at him with the only the briefest curiosity. Oddly, the bagpipe works here, filling the dingy underground space in the intervals between trains with the sounds of the Scottish highlands. The eerie resonance echoes in the subway tunnel. I wonder if the music makes him homesick. I put a quarter in his plastic bowl but he doesn't acknowledge it.

Two Dollar

On the E Train to Continental Avenue there is a peddler, a guy I think I've seen a couple of times. He starts a couple of cheap, battery driven toys and puts them on the floor of the moving subway car—a funny-car that rears up and changes directions; a pig that jumps rope; a bear that beats a drum. He balances himself near the double doors at the center of the car and demonstrates a flashing yo-yo that he takes from one of several worn shopping bags he's placed at his feet. "Two dollar", he says, "two dollar". Then he holds up a toy cellular telephone which beeps electronically and sounds like a real telephone: a sound which cuts through the sound of the moving train. A sound which demands that you look up. "Two dollar", he repeats. Except for some little kids, people work at avoiding paying any attention. The man is expressionless, un-readable, all business; nobody seems to think his performance is funny, he least of all. I worry about the toys getting stepped on, but people just move their feet, and minimally at that, when a toy bumps into them. I think they're relieved at the relatively soft sell.

Duet

A couple of teenagers—a boy and a girl—are standing face to face. It's six-thirty in the evening on the Manhattan bound E. All the commuter traffic is going the other way—out from the city at the end of the evening rush hour. You can see how packed the outbound trains are flashing by in the dark. The car is almost empty and there are seats but these kids are standing.

Both are wearing dirty green parkas, their boots unlaced, carrying what I assume are their schoolbooks in their backpacks. He's leaning back against the door. She's leaning into him. She's kissing his face, which is round and dimpled. There's something exaggerated in their movement and in their expressiveness—especially by contrast to the inwardness of the other riders. Then I see: they're deaf and communicating in sign.

She's signing; kissing and signing. He's answering with his eyebrows. He looks sleepy; even so, his face has a mobility. Her hands are so busy she could be describing butterflies. She's touching his face, signing, touching, kissing. He looks (how to put this?) amused, tolerant. He looks loved. He's responding, agreeing with everything she says—with his eyebrows.

They're still on the train, absorbed in each other, still standing like that, even though there are lots of seats, when I get off at Spring Street. I come up the stairs and out on the west side of Sixth Avenue. The evening is bitter cold. Between the buildings, the sky over the river is a luminous blue, blue when everything else is already black, blue over the river you can't see but know is there.

For a Friend Who Likes to Think His Dead Father Is Watching Over Him

Parental supervision never was an easy thing:
How close to follow behind? When to intervene?
I don't know about your old man, but mine
would need to pick up something in the crossing over
—like a new kind of sensitivity
to what his progeny needs: some of us
just have to make our own mistakes;
others are dying to be saved.

Let's suppose a live one like you or me
is at the wheel of his own late model Chevy.
He's approaching a dangerous intersection,
(close to home, where the accidents typically take place)
going south. A panel truck with faulty brakes
is coming fast and west. Now, there's a stirring
of discomfort in the afterworld; a dead father,
like yours or mine, looks up from his heavenly nap,
and now a message is being sent:

The driver, on the hairs at the back of his neck,
feels something like a breeze. On the radio
a sort of static interrupts the love song
that takes him back to college days. *Something*
tells him to slow down—although the light is his.
But if he thinks at all, he thinks, Why should I?
And then: there's an ambulance & flashing lights,
tow trucks, and they're picking up the pieces.

Now the driver is a new recruit:
After a transitional interval, a consciousness
new & pure, like the dawning of a light,
lights things up for him. At last, a wisdom!
And suitably robed and mantled, he joins
the heavenly panel. I see him shaking
whatever he uses for a head—the way my father did.
He frowns in the puzzled way my father frowned.
He concentrates. (As for the promise of eternal rest,
forget it, as we say on Earth.) It's his job now,
and forever, to keep an eye on all his progeny—
on all the innocents, but no less, the guilty:
Alive & kicking. Not dead yet. No plans to be.

Lost Chord

It's somewhere in the Bronx—there still, and you can't tell
when or if it's ending, like a distant siren echoing in the colonnades
& over the rising ranks of grey stone steps outside the Courthouse,
or the sound the wind makes in a summer storm in the leaves
of the trees in Franz Sigel Park. Or the traffic on the Concourse—
like the tenor hum of the Number 1, the way it sort of sang
when we went uptown by bus to Alexander's. Or heard
the way we heard it on the sidewalk outside Feldmann's,
or on the latest 45 on somebody's Victrola and all of us
were dancing the Lindy in the livingroom when her parents weren't home.
It could be in the air outside the ice cream parlor across from Poe Park
the way it was when I went there with Diana, after the movies
on what we had agreed would be a "date", and she ordered a ham-
    burger
and an ice cream soda and I had the money to pay for one but not
    the other
and we were wearing the matching outfits she had insisted on—
sweaters and the same pink shirts. One night we stayed up
making out so late we decided to wait and see the sunrise from her
    rooftop
and the next day there were some apologies & explanations
we were made to make—but, all things considered, what we said
was true and we *were* chaste. It hung there in the air above
the damp tarpaper, above the empty clotheslines tied to metal stanchions.
An angel—if there were such a thing it would have been there—
could have sight-read the music from above, the clotheslines a kind
    of staff,
the clothespins quavers on it. A chorus of innocents
might have sung it then, then held the final fading chord, holding it,
holding it, as long as their breath might last.

www.ingramcontent.com/pod-product-compliance
Lightning Source LLC
Chambersburg PA
CBHW070548300426
44113CB00011B/1826